PURPOSE: Unmasking and Maximizing Your Inborn Resources to Fulfill Life's Purpose

James s. Fabiyi

Book Layout

Introduction

TABLE OF CONTENTS

Acknowledgements

I would like to thank God for giving me the grace and opportunity to write this important book titled PURPOSE: Unmasking and Maximizing Your Inborn Resources to Fulfill Life's Purpose.

I sincerely appreciate a number of people who encouraged me to write this book. My wife and daughter are my greatest encouragers and motivators, without their support and sacrifices, this book would have not been written. Esther Adamu (nee Afolabi) was helpful by suggesting various things that I could do to make this book widely acceptable by the readers.

I am indebted to the following people who reviewed this book for content editing: Donna Bil (B.Ed.) for reading and editing the entire chapters several times. I cannot thank her enough for her words of encouragement and commendation that the book is the need of the hour. Rev. Del Herman also contributed a lot by editing and his critique of the book. Victor Ademola Adebayo did a great job by designing the beautiful cover of this book; thank you so much.

Targeted Readers

Once upon a time, a man in his twenties had a desire to change the world. He spent almost two decades struggling to accomplish his goal but failed. Then he realized that in order to change the world he had to change his continent. So he settled for changing his continent which he failed to achieve after several years. A thought came to him that if he had changed his country, his country would have changed his continent and his continent would have changed the world. He therefore planned to change his country. After several years of pursuing that he failed. Realizing the futility of his efforts, he changed his mind and focused on changing his province. This plan failed too. Thereafter he made up his mind to change his village but failed to accomplish that too. Finally, he concluded that he would focus on changing himself but it was too late. He was already 100 years old. He died without achieving any of his goals in this life.

This story reveals that strategic planning is a key to great accomplishment in life. Indeed, proper preparation prevents poor performance. If the man had galvanized his youthful energy on changing himself, he would have been able to change his family while his family would have changed his village, the village would have changed the province, the province would have changed the country and the country would have changed the continent while the continent would have changed the world. When people do not know what to do at the appropriate time, all efforts exerted to carry out a right goal will result in failure. Meaningful success starts when a person looks inward to discover the God-given resources that have been deposited in them during their youthful days.

Growing old only to realize what one should have done when one was young is of no use. Another reality of life is that everyone must make hay while the sun shines. So discovery of the inborn resources and matching them with careers at a younger age can help a person navigate through life with focus and less stress. It can be easy to galvanize youthful energy to pursue the right things at the right time.

Therefore, this book will help high school students choose the right careers to pursue before entering colleges or universities. It will also help the college and university students to rethink and refocus their efforts on the appropriate careers that fit their talents. If there are any college and university students who have already chosen a career that does not match their talents, such individuals can change careers if possible. However, if it is not possible because of nearing graduation, remedial training is an alternative way to go. In 2008, I called a friend who had a Ph.D. in agricultural engineering. I counseled him that instead of doing a post-doctoral research program that he should go for a remedial program in business school. I knew that there are few universities that offer the program. The reason for advising him was based on my perception about his talents. He agreed and did it for almost a year. It was not long after he graduated from the business program that he got an assistant professorship job at a college. This job has taken him to many countries outside the United States of America. He is teaching what he likes to do which is business.

This book can also be used by mentors, teachers at all educational levels, counselors, parents and grandparents, uncles and aunts, Sunday school teachers, youth ministers, and pastors to help mentor youth who look up to them as pathfinders.

Welcome on board the flight which will take you on a discovery journey to find your innate resources, and which will result in a safe landing at the fulfillment of your life's purpose. In this flight, Captain Honesty is your pilot. You need to be honest with yourself by strictly following the instructions and key points that are contained in this book. Your flight attendants throughout this journey are the inborn resources — Talents and Uniqueness. In this flight, there are life-strengthening and energy-giving menus which include passion, optimization, and strategy. Although reaching the final destination is energy consuming and stressful, these menus may help you lessen the pain. Evaluation is the security screener that will conduct the final assessment to help you know your admissibility into the expected final destination, which is the fulfillment of your life's purpose. You are either declared successful or advised to repeat the journey. The only way for you not to repeat the journey is to pay attention to every detail contained in this book from the first to the last page. So, fasten your seat belts and get ready for a life-changing flight.

Introduction

"But this precious treasure - this light and power that now shine within us - is held in a perishable container, that is, in our weak bodies."

There is a story told about an eaglet that was raised by a farmer among the chickens. As the eaglet grew, it walked like a chicken, ran like a chicken, cackled like a chicken, scratched and scrambled in the earth with its claws for food like a chicken. It kept on behaving like a chicken. Whenever the eaglet saw any eagle flying in the air looking for prey, the eaglet would run and hide for dear life like the other chickens. In reality, it was not a chicken, but the circumstances of its life made it live like a chicken. The growth process of this eaglet resulted in it growing wings and a long sharp beak that differentiated it from the chickens. The eaglet began to realize that there were similarities between itself and the eagles that flew overhead. Nevertheless, the chickens kept telling the eaglet that it was only a chicken and that it should not compare itself to the eagles. They told it that it was earth-bound and not sky-bound. One day, an old farmer was passing by and saw the eaglet among the chickens. The man was very sad and pitied the eaglet. So he picked it up and went to a very high cliff and threw the eaglet over so it would have to struggle in the air for survival, and thereby discover what it really was. How scary for the eaglet! As it struggled for survival, an instinct came over it and it began to flap its wings. In a short while, the effort began to yield positive results and it was able to fly high into the sky like other eagles.

The eaglet did not know that it was born to fly. In the same way, many people do not know that they are naturally and carefully designed, wired by God and brought into this world to overcome every obstacle of life that might stand against them, including social, environmental, political, family, educational, and financial challenges. Everyone is born to fly far above the principalities and powers that might be in place to suppress them. Every human being is created to bud and bloom. Everyone is born to develop and become stronger, to flourish, and to produce or yield blossoms (see Genesis 1:28). Other creations of God are waiting expectantly for your manifestation as a great scientist, an outstanding surgeon, an accomplished teacher, a great inventor, or a wonderful music composer and performer (Romans 8:19). Every individual created by God is endowed and empowered to bear fruit, to bring forth much fruit, and to bear lasting fruit (John 15:2,15,16). You are not here on earth by accident. You were created to live out a specific course of action to benefit mankind. Therefore, no one has any tenable excuse for not blooming.

There are three major ingredients that need to be put in place for anyone to operate and function to the maximum in their life. The first thing is to have a strong desire to discover the resources that have been purposefully deposited in them by God. No one else can discover them for you. Also, you must not stop at this discovery. You must be motivated to act, to launch into the deep, or to get out of the boat and walk upon the water. Consider the analogy of a good and delicious food that is well prepared and ready to be eaten, but if you do not have an appetite, you may not want to eat it. If you decide to eat it, you may not value or taste it. Likewise, despite the fact that God has deposited in you all the necessary resources you need to bloom, a lack of desire will make you inactive. Remember that no action results in no achievement. Only a hungry and thirsty person will be filled.

There was a man named Paul, who counted all that was gained by him as loss and his desire to bloom caused him to passionately pursue his goal, which resulted in a miraculous ministry for God (Philippians 3:12-15). Likewise the desire to bloom made Isaac sow seeds in a foreign country when many foreigners did not want to sow seeds there for various reasons (Gen. 26:12-14). Isaac was rewarded with a hundredfold harvest.

The second ingredient that a person needs to bloom is to be confident and believe that God has deposited in him all the necessary qualities to excel. The slogan of the man running for office who became the first African-American President of the United States of America was "yes we can." You can do all things and become anything that you desire with the help of God and with unrelenting effort and hard work. Develop the habit of saying "I can do it" and drop the slogan of saying "I cannot do it." If you believe in yourself, all things will be possible for you.

The third ingredient is to develop a concrete strategy and a workable plan to use your inborn resources. Indeed, no one would want to go to war with the goal of defeating his or her opponent without first determining his or her military strength. Similarly, no one would want to build an edifice without first counting what it would cost. So, people first need to map out all the necessary steps they need to take to bloom in their lives and careers. Then the workability and achievability of the plan depends on their determination and discipline to keep pressing on even when it seems like nothing is happening. Similarly, manually producing gravel (small stones) may be discouraging at first as you begin to hit the rock with a hammer, but remember that it takes time for the rock to begin to break into pebbles.

In this book, the correlation between life's purpose and career is explained. Emphasis is laid on the fact that everyone is uniquely talented to bloom in this world. The steps needed to discover every individual's talents and uniqueness and how to maximize their use are described by using every letter of the word P-U-R-P-O-S-E. In this case, the first three letters, P-U-R, stand for Potential, Uniqueness, and Reflection. How to know if what is discovered is truly from God is addressed. Additionally, how to match the discovered inborn resources with a possible career choice is considered. Then, the last four letters, P-O-S-E, stand for Passion, Optimization, Strategy, and Evaluation are considered as principles for fulfilling and maximizing the use of any discovered inborn resources.

PART I

INBORN RESOURCES VS LIFE'S PURPOSE

Chapter 1

Inborn Resources and Life's purpose

"I have fought a good fight, I have finished my course, ...
Henceforth there is laid up for me a crown of righteousness, ..." -
Paul

At one time the Jews were faced with a big challenge in the Persian kingdom.. It was clear that without a deliverer to intervene on their behalf, they would all be killed. Fortunately for them at the time, one of the Jewish daughters, Esther, a slave girl, became queen to the King of Persia. When her uncle, Mordecai, heard about the plot against the Jews, he sent a messenger to Queen Esther to intervene on their behalf. Esther was afraid because the law, once signed, could not be changed (see Daniel 6:8). Therefore, she rejected the request. When Mordecai was told about the fear that Esther had, he sent this message to her: "... Maybe you were made queen for just such a time as this" (Esther 4:12-14 MSG). The fact is, every man or woman is created to carry out a responsibility on earth using his or her natural ability, profession or position. Literally, this does not mean that one's assignment is to do what no other person has done. It is important to note that there is a clear difference between responsibility (life's purpose) and natural ability (inborn resources).

Life's purpose is simply defined as the primary reason for human existence in the world. It is the principal motivating aim of the Creator of life for all human beings. Once life's purpose is realized, people's decision-making would be guided appropriately, life principles and behavioral orientation would be shaped, and life goals as well as attitude to secular and spiritual life would be well directed. Unlike life's purpose, inborn resources are the natural abilities of a person known as talents and uniqueness. The difference between the two could be best explained by considering the misconceptions about life's purpose.

Misconception #1: Life's purpose is all about a particular job, career, or vocation.

From the account of Queen Esther, she might be thinking that her life's purpose is to be a queen and just carry out her queenly duties. Indeed, her life's purpose was much more than that. She was a queen (position or career) at such a time so as to be a helper and deliverer (rescuer — life's purpose) of the Jews from their looming destruction. Without being a queen, she would not have had the opportunity to be a deliverer for the Jews at such a moment. In addition, a man named Daniel became an influential and accomplished advisor to various kings in Babylon for almost 70 years during the exile of the Israelites, because of the extraordinary spirit of wisdom that God gave him (Daniel 1:19-20; 6:3). He used his wisdom and office (talent and position) to testify (life's purpose) to the greatness, goodness and rulership of God.

There are lots of medical doctors who earn big salaries, happily working as healthcare providers, but not having a sense of fulfillment in life. However, some Christians engage in the same profession, but also use it to help their patients discover God and experience Christ's love. Such Christian doctors are fulfilling their life's purpose in their profession.

Therefore, from the account of Esther and Daniel, as well as the analogy of the medical doctors, it is clear that job, career, or vocation serve as a vehicle through which life's purposes can be accomplished.

Misconception #2: Every individual has a life's purpose that differs from others, and which can only be fulfilled in a specific career.

The reality about a vocation or career is that a person can perform well in multiple professions. Again, the analogy of the medical doctors is still relevant. For instance, someone can be a good medical doctor if that is the career that they choose. However, the same person may be very good as a science or mathematics teacher. In any of the career paths that such a person chooses, life's purpose can still be fulfilled and provide internal joy and eternal reward.

For instance, when I was a university teacher, I believed that I had a life's purpose within that profession to be an ambassador of Christ. Now that I am a full-time pastor, I know that I have a life's purpose to fulfill to the congregation that I serve, to the community where I live, and to the entire world, by living as an ambassador of Christ. Though the two environments (careers) are different, my life's purpose still remains the same - to glorify God.

Therefore, an individual can function well in various careers, and yet carry out their life's purpose in any chosen career. The resources to function effectively and efficiently in any career come from inborn talents and uniqueness. Realizing these resources to fulfill life's purpose is very important. If the resources available to a person to fulfill life's purpose are unknown, it could lead to an abuse of life. However, when we know our inborn resources, it helps us to have a focus. A person with no direction has many directions, and lives a messy life by becoming a "Jack of all trades and a master of none."

Once we discover our inborn resources, it becomes an investment of treasure and time. Our energy becomes well-directed and applied to fulfill our life's purpose. When a God-given resource is discovered, the use of such a resource gives room for self-assessment, and provides a tool to monitor progress or failure.

So far, the difference between the inborn resources — talents and uniqueness — and life's purpose has been clearly explained. Talents and uniqueness help a person to excel in his or her career. Though a person can do well in many careers in life, life's purpose is to be fulfilled in whichever career the person chooses. For you to better realize your life's purpose, the next chapter is written to address it.

CHAPTER 2
Your Life's purpose

"Even every one that is called by my name: for I have created him for my glory, I have formed him; yea, I have made him."[2] (Isaiah 43:7)

There are lots of books and articles that have been written and lots of conferences and workshops held on the importance of discovering and fulfilling life's purpose. Unfortunately, most of these books and events do not clarify what life's purpose is all about. I have heard many people say that they are praying to know God's purpose for their existence. After my reading through the Bible from Genesis to Revelation, I find that it was only the Apostle Paul who asked, "Lord, what do You want me to do?" (Acts 9:6). Then the Lord said to him, "Arise and go into the city, and you will be told what you must do." The answer that the Lord's messenger brought is amazing and universal, as well as one of the two purposes why God created every individual on earth. One of the reasons that could make people think that we should pray to know our life's purpose is the lack of an understanding of the difference between God's will and God's purpose for us.

Jesus taught His disciples a model of prayer when He said "Your will be done, on earth as it is in heaven" (Matthew 6:10 NIV). The Greek words "*thelema, boulema* and *prosthesis*" mean "will, plan and purpose," respectively.

The "will" means desire, wish, or delight. "Plan" means a detailed proposal for achieving something while "purpose" means a target or a goal to be reached. God's desire (will) is that all human beings may be saved (1 Timothy 2:4) and His plan was to send Jesus Christ to die for the sins of mankind (Genesis 3:15; John 1:29). So God created men and women and deposited some inborn resources in them so that we would become tools to achieve His target (purpose) (Ezekiel 3:17; Acts 26:12-19). God's will refers to the concept of God having a desire for everyone to be involved in a certain duty or career at a certain time in order to fulfill His purpose. God has disclosed His will in the Bible, "and the things that have been revealed in the Bible belong to us and to our children forever. We must obey every word of these teachings" (Deut. 29:29 GW). It is therefore our responsibility to ask God to reveal His hidden will to us.

We can ask several questions. Which profession or occupation should I pursue? Which university should I choose? Whom should I marry? What should I do in a specific time? The reason for asking these questions is that we want to know God's Will concerning the issues of life. So we need to pray to know God's will (Colossians 1:19). Saul of Tarsus was asking the Lord (Acts 9:6) what office the Lord wanted him to occupy to fulfill his life's purpose. We only need to study the Bible and the other creations of God to know our life's purpose.

Nature declares the majesty of God. People can look for what is hidden but need to act on what is already revealed. Every individual has a purpose in life. However, each profession or occupation differs from person to person. Generally speaking, life's purposes could easily be put into two groups according to creation and the Bible.

Endorsing God

The first and foremost purpose in life for all human beings is endorsement. According to the Cambridge English Dictionary, to endorse is to make a public statement of support for something or someone. Therefore, our talents and uniqueness are public proof of God's incomprehensible creative design. Every human being is a testament to how uniquely God created and deposited various talents in us. Indeed, everyone who is called human is formed to showcase the greatness and glory of God, since our talents bring praise to Him (Isaiah 43:7,21; 1 Corinthians 10:31).

Wait a minute! Are you thinking that only Christians are to be witnesses? Let's consider whether or not non-Christians can witness! Have you seen an athlete that is highly talented and excellent in his career? If yes, then have you noticed that after displaying his athletic ability and performing brilliantly, the spectators cheer him, making exclamatory remarks that God has given him such a wonderful talent? Some could even wish that God would give them such talent. At such a moment, what do you think people are doing? The talent in the life of the athlete showcases him and directs people's attention to God's creative wisdom and power. I agree that non-Christians may deny the fact that it is God who has endowed them with talents, but their denial holds no water. King David wrote, "The heavens are telling the glory of God; they are a marvelous display of his craftsmanship. Day and night they keep on telling about God. Without a sound or word, silent in the skies, their message reaches out to the entire world. The sun lives in the heavens where God placed it and moves out across the skies as radiant as a bridegroom going to his wedding, or as joyous as an athlete looking forward to a race! The sun crosses the heavens from end to end, and nothing can hide from its heat" (Psalm 19:1-4 LTB).

Equipping others

The second reason why we exist on earth is to equip others to rise up and become what God wants them to be. According to the Cambridge Dictionary, to equip is "to give someone the skills required to carry out a particular task." After we have discovered our natural ability and become a master of it, it is our responsibility to help others discover and put to use their own natural ability too. The main goal is help others gain stability and steadfastness and learn to use their own talent to benefit mankind.

Plato, a renowned philosopher, gave an analogy entitled "The Allegory of the Cave" in which he wrote about the importance of education and enlightenment. Let us quote directly from a book called "The Republic."

> "Imagine human beings living in an underground den which is open towards the light. They have been there from childhood, having their necks and legs chained, and can only see into the den. At a distance there is a fire, and between the fire and the prisoners is a raised way, and a low wall is built along the way, like the screen over which marionette players show their puppets. Behind the wall appear moving figures, who hold in their hands various works of art, and among them images of men and animals made of wood and stone. Some of the passers-by are talking and others are silent. They see only the shadows of the

images which the fire throws on the wall of the den. To these they give names, and if we add an echo which returns from the wall, the voices of the passengers will seem to proceed from the shadows. Imagine that they are dragged up a steep and rugged ascent into the presence of the sun. Would not their sight be darkened with the excess of light? Some time will pass before they are able to see at all. At first they will be able to perceive only shadows and reflections in the water, and then they will recognize the moon and the stars, and will at length be able to behold the sun in its own proper place..."

Plato finally concluded that the freed prisoner would, out of pity for the other prisoners, go back to rescue them so that they too could experience the sunlight.

From the allegory, the world, human beings, and ignorance are represented by the cave, the prisoners, and the chains that prevent the prisoners from escaping, respectively. The sunlight is the marvelous work of God waiting to be discovered. The person that first escaped from the cave has used his talent and uniqueness to discuss the work of God. Those who were still in chains in the cave are people who have not discovered their own talents and uniqueness.

Therefore, Plato's cave allegory represents the importance of equipping others with information that will help them discover the potential that is embedded in them which could help them fulfill their life's purpose. Indeed, every successful person, in the use of each career or talent, is to help others discover their own careers or talents. There are several ways through which effective mentors equip others to become effective users of their talents. No matter which approach is used, treasure, training, tools, and time are the four basic ingredients that must be considered. Mentors help mentees discover the treasure (talent) in them. They purposefully invest time to train mentees by providing the needed tools that will aid in coaching them effectively.

Equipping others is a process and the best example of how this process works is evidenced in Christ's equipping strategies. It is written that "Jesus went up on a mountainside and called to him those he wanted, and they came to him. He appointed twelve that they might be with Him and that He might send them out to preach and to have authority to drive out demons" (Mark 3:13-15 NIV). Let us break down these strategies as follows:

See: Among the twelve disciples that Jesus called, the first four were in the fishing business before becoming Christ's disciples. He told them that instead of fishing for fish, they would begin to fish for men. In a way, He opened their eyes to see a greater business into which they could put their fishing talent. Therefore, after someone has gained mastery in a talent, their life's purpose should be to help others discover their own talents too. He must use diverse approaches to help others identify their talents and uniqueness.

Say: After Jesus had called the twelve, He made His intention known — "that they might be with Him and that He might send them out to preach and to have authority to drive out demons." Once an achiever has helped others see what talents they possess, he needs to explain the importance of using their talents. He then needs to tell them the various steps to take to put such talents into maximum use to benefit mankind.

Show: Jesus called these disciples to be with Him. He wanted them to see how He did things, demonstrating to them how divine assignments were to be carried out. He showed them how they would need to perform the assigned responsibilities through the use of their talents.

Steer: In the course of equipping His disciples, Jesus sent them out to practice what they had learned from Him. It is the life's purpose of every achiever not only to show people what they need to do, but to let them try doing it on their own. A good mentor would allow the mentee to practice, allowing them to exercise their sense of reasoning in the achievement process.

Support: For the learners to make maximum gain, the equipper must be there in the early stages to watch when they are using their talents. Applaud them when they do well. Give them future direction and come alongside them in their journey of discovery and use of their natural ability.

Survey: At the end of the first assignment Jesus gave to a group of seventy disciples, they came to Him and explained all that had happened in the course of using their "talents" when performing the assigned responsibilities. Then He offered His feedback and said that greater accomplishment awaited them than the success they had just recorded. Therefore, every mentor has a responsibility to give constructive criticism to the mentee with the goal of ensuring better performance in any future attempt.

In summary, this chapter reveals that the main purposes of everyone's life are to be a witness to the creativeness of God and to use their natural endowments to equip others to discover and use their inborn resources. Further clarification of inborn resources and the tools needed to discover them are considered in the next chapter.

CHAPTER 3
Discovery of Inborn Resources

No human being is poorly designed by God; what
people call deficiency is made up for in other areas.
When those areas are discovered and developed
efficiently, we then refer to them as talents

Imagine a parent with two children. One is naturally smart at school as an A+ student and ends up becoming a medical doctor. The second child performs poorly at school and ends up dropping out. This parent is known for praising the A+ child and comparing him to the seemingly poor child, telling the poor child that he would not become an important person in life because of his poor academic performance. However, one thing that this parent failed to see is that the academically poor child had a very strong creative imagination. He spent most of his time designing and building various technological devices. In spite of having had no good formal education, he became an inventor of many outstanding technological devices, including those that would help medical doctors carry out effective and more accurate diagnoses of their patients' illnesses.

In a similar analogy, left-handed children in the past have often been stigmatized, sometimes classified as having an abnormality. Conversely, according to Cherbuin and Brinkman (2006), quicker information processing is associated with faster connections between the right and left hemispheres of the brain in left-handed people. This could give them an upper hand in things like video games and sports. In addition, because the brains of lefties have a more highly developed right hemisphere, which is strongly involved in creative thinking, they are creative by nature.

Therefore, the truth is that no human being is poorly designed by God. What we call a deficiency in a person's life is made up for in other areas. When those areas are discovered and developed efficiently, we then refer to them as talents. Unfortunately, many people accept the deficiency stigma because they fail failure to discover the hidden, undeveloped talents they possess. This book is written to enlighten everyone in the steps to take to discover the specific, naturally deposited resources we have to fulfill our life's purposes. As we are about to take a journey of discovery of individual specific inborn resources, we must realize that we are not equally blessed with resources, talents, and uniqueness. One person may be more talented than another, but that does not mean that the person with less talent is less important than the person with many talents. Jesus once told His followers a parable of a man who went on a journey to a far country. He handed his properties over to his three servants to manage for him. To the first servant he gave five talents (say about $5,000), to the second he gave two talents (say $2,000) and to the third he gave one talent (say $1,000). They were supposed to go and trade their varying talents and come back with a profit. Unfortunately, the third servant was not happy to have been given only one talent when the first and second servants had been given five and two respectively. So he refused to put his talents into use (Matthew 25:14-31). He was blamed for not using his talents.

There is a common saying that rich people will keep on becoming richer while the poor will become poorer. If you are not happy because you think that your own talent is small in size or quantity compared to that of another person, and you refuse to make use of it, remember that as a result you will remain unproductive and poor. You will lose what you don't use. So, use it or lose it.

We must realize that God's purpose for us must be accomplished individually by using the available resources needed for it. When everyone uses their talent, it brings blessings to our world. If a person does not use his or her own inborn resources, such failure would cause more burdens on the people who are using their own resources to fill the gap in the collective purpose. Others will have to struggle harder for survival because of that individual's refusal to be useful to society. The same applies to various organizations. We all need each other irrespective of the size of the talent of each individual. The philosophy of systems thinking reveals that every part of the system matters. The fingers are tiny in size compared to the whole body while the mouth is just a relatively small door into the entire body. However, if the fingers refuse to function because of comparing themselves to bigger body parts, the other parts would have to struggle to grab things, especially food to put into the mouth. If the mouth refuses to open for the food to enter because of an inferiority complex, it is likely then that the whole body would die of starvation without any medical intervention (1 Corinthians 12:15-26). The point is, do not refuse to put your talent into use regardless of whether or not you think it is significant. You may need to strive to discover your talent.

Since we are examining how to (1) find the inborn resources and (2) how to use them to fulfill life's purpose, it is quite fascinating to just chunk the word PURPOSE into the appropriate syllables - **PUR** and **POSE**. "Pur" is equivalent to "pro" which means before. "**Pose**" simply means assuming a particular attitude or position in order to be photographed. It means getting ready for action. Therefore, combining the two words, **PUR** and **POSE**, based on our topic of consideration, connotes finding inborn resources and then getting ready to use them. With this understanding, let us employ the acronym of the word "**P.U.R.P.O.S.E.**" to unravel the steps to discover and develop the inborn resources.

> ➢ **P - Potential**
> ➢ **U - Uniqueness**
> ➢ **R - Reflection**
> ➢ **P - Passion**
> ➢ **O - Optimization**
> ➢ **S - Strategy**
> ➢ **E - Evaluation**

It is clear from this section that God created everyone to fulfill their ordained life's purpose which is endorsing God and equipping others through the use of the resources that the Creator has deposited in them. The next three chapters are based on the use of **P**otential, **U**niqueness and **R**eflection to find the inborn resources in every individual.

PART II

FINDING YOUR INBORN RESOURCES USING P-U-R

CHAPTER 4
Potential

There is a true story told of a rich man who had a son in whom he was highly delighted. In his final year at college, the boy desired a particular sports car as his graduation gift from his father. The sports car had been his dream car for a long time and he told his father what he wanted. Indeed, it was affordable for his father. One day, as the graduation got near, his father called him and presented him with a well-packaged gift box. The boy was not sure what the father had wrapped inside the box. He opened it and found a Bible with his name embossed on the cover in gold. He was disappointed that his father would give him a Bible instead of the sports car that he had requested. He angrily went away from his father, leaving the Bible behind and he did not return home. After some years had passed, his father died without ever seeing his son again. However, before his father died, he had willed his property and wealth to the son. When the son came back to claim all that his father had willed to him, as he was going through everything in the house, he saw the Bible, still brand new as he had left it. Curiously, he opened it and started flipping through the pages of the Bible. When he opened it to a certain Scripture, because his father had underlined a verse there, he decided to read what it contained. As he was reading, a car key dropped from the back of the Bible. The tag on the key had the name of the car dealer who carried the sports car that he had wanted. Additional information on the tag said "paid in full."

The young man would not have needed to struggle to buy his dream sports car if he had opened the Bible and flipped through it when the gift was given to him. Dear readers, many people are like the young man. We have a special, desirable gift, well wrapped and packaged, but we refuse to unwrap it because it is not packed the way we want. Unfortunately, many people do not even discover the hidden treasure inside them. It is just like Gideon, who did not realize the potential in him until he was told by an angel that he had great skill to be an unconquerable warrior (Judges 6:13).

A person's potential is the inborn ability deposited in him or her. According to the Lexico Dictionary, potential (noun) is the latent (silent, underdeveloped, dormant) quality or ability that may be developed and lead to future success or usefulness. In addition, potential is a natural ability which one can develop. Every created person on earth has one or more potentialities embedded in them. They are hidden, unrealized, and untapped capabilities which are developed through use to benefit mankind. However, until such potentialities are discovered, embraced, and developed, a very talented person may live an untalented life and die without any achievement at all. There were many people who were talented to be great authors of many inspiring and life-transforming books, but died without writing a single one. There were many people who were talented to be good and great athletes, endowed to win many gold medals and trophies, yet they died without displaying any athletic ability. There were many people who were naturally talented for mathematics but died without solving any simple algebraic or mathematical equations. There were many people who were talented with inquisitive and innovative minds but died without inventing any philosophical, scientific, or technological inventions that would have benefited them and/or humanity. Why would such people die without impacting their generations with their talents when God has deposited such treasures in them? The answer is that some of them discovered their talents, but did not develop them, or they may never have discovered them at all.

The truth is that every individual is fearfully and wonderfully created. It can be deduced that talent is one of the wonderful things that God has deposited in every person. Your ethnicity, color of skin, gender, or age does not matter. Everyone has talents that are embedded in them at birth. Therefore, every person is a talented person. Some talents include intelligence, physical strength, organization, athletics, writing, design, drawing, painting, sculpturing, pottering, performing arts, acting, music, singing, photography, science, gardening, and public speaking. The list is endless.

There is a common African adage which says that "he who wants to have honey that is under the rock would not worry about the blade of his axe." This means that it takes diligence, perseverance, and relentless effort to discover a gem. Therefore, know for sure that every individual has well-wrapped and well-packaged inborn resources waiting to be unwrapped. What every individual needs to succeed in life is inside of him. You may need to be diligent and persevering to unwrap and flip through from one page to another until the talent is discovered. The question is, how can we discover our God-given talents? In order to embark on this discovery journey, the following guidelines are very helpful.

Step One: Ask Heart-Probing Questions

Find and stay in a quiet place where you can ask yourself some heart-probing questions which will help you discover your inborn resources. By all means, avoid distractions or any wandering thoughts. Have your pen and paper ready to write down whatever answers that may come to your mind as you consider the following questions.

Question 1: What are my talents?

Every human being has been endowed with special, natural strengths and talents. It is important to write down a list of all the things that you are really good at, which come naturally to you.

These include all the activities that friends or co-workers have been telling you that you are very good at doing (i.e. good listener, hospitality, leadership). Write down all the things that you do really well at home, from the past or in the present (e.g. organizing, landscaping, care-giving, etc.)

Question 2: What are you passionate about?

"For where your treasure is, there your heart will be also" (Matthew 6:21 NIV). Whatever you are passionate about will give you inner strength and energy. Therefore, the following approaches will help you identify what you are passionate about.

1. Write down all your favorite activities that you have engaged in within the last ten years. This list could also include the favorite activities that are still fascinating to you, and beg for your attention.
2. Which of these activities make you consider time as immaterial?

   Many of these activities would probably be from those that you have written down as your favorites. Do not write any activity that bores you but rather those that make you lose track of time.

A story told about Isaac Newton is that he skipped meals and sleep for many years because he was busy in the laboratory making lots of scientific discoveries. So, any activity that makes you forget about checking the time is what you treasure. Most of the time, as you engage in such an activity, you forget about your lunch, or even an appointment. You are completely immersed in what you are doing. Note, when something is boring to you, time becomes too long.

3. Which activities make you feel great about yourself?

   Ask yourself which activities make you feel proud of yourself when you do them? Which one makes you feel that wow, I have something to be proud of, or something to offer? Remember, these could still include those that you have written before.

4. Which activities are you excited to always think and talk about?

   If you were given an opportunity to teach a group of people about an activity, which of these activities would you be delighted in and excited to talk about?

   As you write your thoughts down, you will notice that you freely operate more in one of the activities or thoughts than the others. For example, if you are to be in the medical field you will see yourself helping the sick. If you are called to be a teacher, you will always envisage yourself teaching students in a classroom. If you are to be in the church ministry, you will always envisage yourself praying, teaching, preaching, counseling, encouraging people, etc.

Question 3: What are the things or activities that you do that bring happiness to other people? These activities are those which are born out of a passion to meet the needs of other people. In order to answer this question, you need to jump to step two.

Step Two: Combine your answers to discover your specific talents

In mathematics, there is an aspect called "set theory" which uses a set diagram commonly known as the "Venn diagram." A Venn diagram is based on the concept mapping approach which uses overlapping circles to display all possible logical relationships between two or more sets of items to determine their similarity or dissimilarity. To find the talents and uniqueness into which you need to invest to make you become outstanding in life, a Venn diagram method can be used.

This method is based on the simple idea of graphically organizing your thoughts into three categories.

1. Something you're good at (talents)
2. Something you enjoy doing, that makes you lose track of time and you are excited to talk about (passion)
3. Something that improves the lives of other people (need-driven activities) and testifies to the great work of God's creation.

The graphical representation of these three categories into a Venn diagram will assist you in narrowing down all your apparent talents and passions into a few on which you should focus your energy. Arrange all the identified activities into where they belong on the Venn diagram. The best talent to fulfill your life's purpose has a high probability of being the one that falls within the intersection of the overlapping circles.

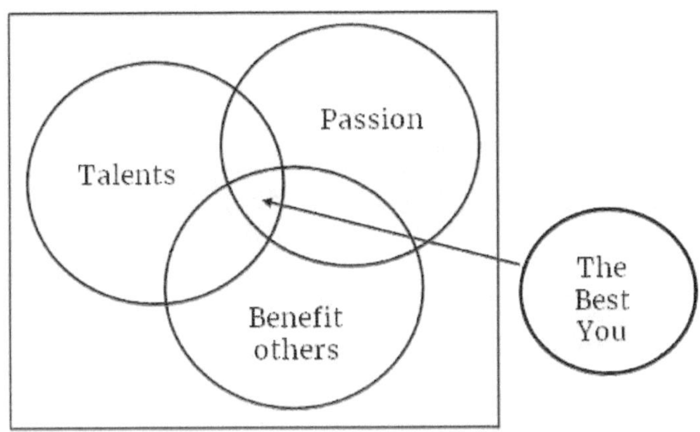

Venn diagram

The combination of these three categories can be used to form a mission statement stating how to use your God-given talents to fulfill your life's purpose.

Using my (inborn resources) to carry out a (need-driven activity) will help me fulfill my life's purpose of endorsing God and equipping humanity.

Consider the following example and then come up with your own:

My teaching ability and my passion for researching information will help me enlighten people to understand the will of God and serve Him wholeheartedly in accordance with Scripture.

Another approach you can use to narrow down all your favorite activities apart from the Venn diagram is the use of Table Format

Questionnaires. Rate each interest using the list in Table 1. Feel free to add others to the list.

5 = Extremely characteristic of me (above 90%)

4 = Most of the time this would describe me (75%)

3 = Often characteristic of me (50%)

2 = Rarely characteristic of me (25%)

1 = Not describe me at all (less than 5%)

In order to discover which of the talents from the questionnaires is your dominant talent, follow these instructions:

1. This questionnaire will help you identify your talents.

2. Every individual has a dominant talent while some people possess more than one.

3. As you read each statement check the most appropriate and most accurate answer. Please be sincere and truthful to yourself.

4. Talent with a point 5 score is your dominant one.

Table 1: Finding your talent assessment protocol

	5	4	3	2	1
Acting – natural ability to enjoy performing at anywhere and at any time.					
Administration – ability to guide, direct, and lead others to perform beyond expectation.					
Artistic talents- ability to draw, paint, sing, and design					
Care-giving – ability to passionately desire and involve in supporting people to be mentally, emotionally, and physically stable and comfortable.					
Coaching – ability to engage in teaching and training others through the acquired skills in a specialized profession.					
Counseling – ability to wisely provide useful and practical solution as regards different circumstances of life.					

Table 1 Contd.: Finding your talent assessment protocol

	5	4	3	2	1
Crafts – ability to enjoy handiwork and making things skilfully with hands.					
Creativity – ability to delightfully provide solutions to problems through innovative idea.					
Decorating: ability to beautify and add value to things with all pleasure.					
Entrepreneur – ability to initiate a new business and start-up from ideation.					
Exhortation – ability to inspire and persuade others to pursue and accomplish their goal.					
Hospitality – ability to lovingly accommodate both strangers and familiar people. Ability to entertain and embrace people while making them to feel at home.					

Table 1 Contd.: Finding your talent assessment protocol

	5	4	3	2	1
Leadership: ability to be a pathfinder, provide solution, instruct others on way to go for greater accomplishment of set goal.					
Mentoring – ability to serve as a good companion, guides, inspire, and help others fulfill their goal by using their knowledge gained and life experiences.					
Music – ability to easily communicate through singing or playing musical instrument.					
Organizing: ability to coordinate events with ease. Ability to ensure that all activities are well-planned and layout without any loopholes.					

Table 1 Contd.: Finding your talent assessment protocol

	5	4	3	2	1
Painting – ability to paint anything to admiration by others.					
Public Relations - ability to share, promote a vision and help it gain acceptance by the targeted consumer.					
Singing: ability to sing melodiously and resonantly					
Story Telling – ability to make stories intrigues, persuasive, fascinating, and admirable in creative ways.					
Teaching – ability to explain complex material or abstract information in simple, concise, clear, easy-to-understand manners.					
Writing – ability to creatively communicate ideas in compelling written style.					

The lists of talents are many and could not be exhausted in this book.

Talents have been considered in this book as hidden potentialities. In addition, two major steps to finding talents were described. The first step deals with the use of heart-probing questions while the second step is based on deducing talents from the answers to those questions. The second letter of P-U-R, which stands for uniqueness, is employed to find inborn resources in the next chapter.

CHAPTER 5
Uniqueness

Everyone has a unique signature, which differentiates
one person from the other. It is a fingerprint. When
others try to copy it, it cannot be exactly the same.

Uniqueness is a common word that means the only one of its
kind. Unfortunately, what many people have written about the
word seems to contradict what we all agree it means. Mostly,
uniqueness is mistakenly taken to be equivalent to talent.
Uniqueness and talent are two different endowments from God
upon people. Talent is not the only one of its kind, and is a natural
ability. Many people can have the same talent. However,
uniqueness cannot be duplicated. It is like a fingerprint, so no two
people can have the same uniqueness.

My wife Rebecca and I are very good at cooking. There is a
particular African snack called puff-puff, which is similar to a
donut, that we like to make. Although our brands have a similar
taste, her brand is unique in its own way and is different from
mine. The texture and softness of Rebecca's brand makes it
enjoyable to eat. When we were in the United States, our African
friends used to call it Rebecca's signature. My brand cannot
compete with that of Rebecca when it comes to texture and
softness, but mine is very unique based on its well-rounded shape
and smooth shell. In fact, whenever my wife tries to make the snack
well-rounded with a smooth shell, the difference is still obvious.

Therefore, when the two brands are set on a table side-by-side,
people will gravitate towards my brand because of its visual

appeal. However, when a person is able to taste the two brands, the person will take Rebecca's brand for a second round because of its texture and softness.

From this scenario, it is clear that both of our brands are unique. Her signature is the texture and softness while my signature is the well-rounded shape and smooth shell. Therefore, uniqueness is not about making a good puff-puff, but it is about the quality of the special touch in its final production. Uniqueness is not about skill as some count it to be. It is about that little finishing touch which makes the product stand out. Skills are developed with practice which makes one person do something differently than the other. Both Rebecca and I are talented in making puff-puffs. Talent is a natural ability to be good at doing something, either with or without being taught. If a group of people undergo training on the piano, for example, talent makes one person learn it faster than the others. However, uniqueness is like a fingerprint which makes a person stands out in the handling of the piano. Indeed, there are many people who have the same talent and skill of playing the piano, but the way of carrying out their own talent or skill is uncommon and incomparable to others. The technique that one person uses to strike the keys on the piano is so fascinating and unique compared to any other instrumentalist. There are many soccer players who are very talented, but their way of handling the soccer ball on the field is unique from one person to another. The way a particular player moves on the field is so unique that spectators like to focus their attention on him. It is common to trace a work of art to a particular artist because of the unique way in which each artist does his own work.

Uniqueness also differentiates how a person perceives things, expresses thoughts, or performs an activity. How can a person find his or her uniqueness?

Step 1: Discover your talent or skill

In order to find your uniqueness, you need to first of all discover your talent because your uniqueness is in your talent. Recall that chapters 4 to 7 of this book deal with how to discover your talents.

Step 2: Find the personal traits that make you unique.

Ask honest associates, the people who have a close relationship with you and have watched you doing what you like to do. Ask them what they notice or think about you that make you stand out from other people.

Be sensitive as to what makes you feel authentic. It could be your style in any of the following areas: public speaking, humour, writing, networking, advertising, drawing, creativity, teaching, learning, reading, coding, persuading, negotiating, singing, doing athletics, performing arts, etc.

It is clear that your uniqueness is manifested in your talent. Many people may possess the same talent that you have, but the unique way in which you display yours differs from others. The last letter of P-U-R, which stands for reflection, will be considered next.

Chapter 6
Reflection

"If a child falls he will look ahead but if an adult falls
he will look back"
• African adage
"Every adversity has the seed of an equivalent or
greater benefit."
• Napoleon Hill, author of *Think and Grow Rich*

Life is full of challenges and celebrations as well as adversities and advancement. Reflecting on the past experiences of life could help people discover a specific pattern of problem solving, or gain an understanding of a certain approach they take in order to have a glorious and fulfilling future. For any individual to gain a mastery of life, it is important to reflect on past experiences, whether they are good or bad, failed or successful, because it teaches a valuable lesson on how to move forward. According to John Dewey, the reason for reflecting on the past is to find the link that "binds together cause and effect, which makes our foresights more accurate and comprehensive." There is a wise saying that experience is the best teacher. Although this is not 100% true in all situations, the experiences of life can be a very useful tool to guide us, or it can become a misleading tool in decision-making or judgement. So, be careful and let God guide your thoughts. God does not primarily orchestrate any steps we have taken to overcome the challenges and adversities of life for our own personal use, but also to benefit mankind.

Our newly discovered potential and uniqueness could be pointers in finding the inborn resources in us. The story of young David who killed Goliath shows how the use of reflection on the challenges of life helped him discover his God-given resource. Saul, who was king over Israel when the Philistines came to fight with the Israelites, told David that he was not able to fight Goliath because of his lack of war experience. However, David reflected on his past experiences, on how he had confronted and fought a lion and a bear that had come to kill the sheep that he was tending. He remembered that he had used a particular technique of targeting the whiskers of these animals before killing them. Through such reflection he came to the conclusion that as he strategically confronted and killed the lion and the bear, so he would apply the same technique to kill Goliath, which he did.

The approach used to overcome an adversity could become a useful resource of hope for millions of people. Writing and teaching other people who may be facing a similar adversity could be of great benefit to them.

There is a common adage by a tribe in Nigeria that says "If a child falls he will look forward but if an adult falls he will look back." The moral of this adage is that an adult will be careful to reflect on past experiences to discover what made him fall in order to avoid making the same mistake in the future. Reflecting back on our past lives could help us discover our ability to face the future. You never know what you have until you take an inventory. The following heart-probing questions will help you discover your God-given resources through reflection.

1. Write down the most complex, tough adversities that you have overcome in your life

2. What steps did you take to overcome each of the listed adversities?

   ❖ Adversity #1:

     Step taken to overcome it:

   ❖ Adversity #2:

     Step taken to overcome it:

   ❖ Adversity #3:

     Step taken to overcome it:

   ❖ Adversity #4:

     Step taken to overcome it:

God may allow the adversities and trials of life that we have experienced to teach us some ways to discover the great natural ability we have to face the future. It could help us in the following areas:

1. To serve as a motivational tool. Your past adversities could make you become an epitome of hope and encouragement to others that are, or will be, facing a similar adversity now or in the future.

2. To gain your attention or redirect you. Take the case of Jonah in the bible. Jonah had a clear vision about where God wanted him to go and the reason why he should go. However, he decided to go in the other direction. Therefore, God used a storm to redirect him (Jonah 1:1-17; 3:1-5).

Reflection is based on heart-probing questions about your past experiences, good or bad, the storms of life, your struggles, and adversities, and how you managed to overcome them. It also based on how you have allowed such experiences to shape you. Indeed, you might have allowed the experiences to make you bitter or better, to mar, or make you. It all depends on your attitude at such a time. Someone says "when life throws you lemons, make lemonade."

Another aspect of reflection is the biography of life. This begins at the start of your life's journey, from childhood to the present day.

1. When I was a child, what did I dream of becoming in life?
2. When I was a child, who was my hero that I tried to emulate?
3. When I was a child, what were the things that excited me most?

Repeat these same questions for when you were in high school, college or University, and finally NOW. Any pattern in solving the challenges of life that you have faced, if harnessed, could be a pointer to what God wants you to use as a resource in life.

Now that we have used P-U-R (potential, uniqueness, reflection) to discover our inborn resources, the next task is to be ready for action by using P-O-S-E (passion, optimization, strategy, evaluation). However, if you are still not sure that the talent and uniqueness that you have discovered is yours, then there is a need for confirmation. The next chapter addresses that.

PART III
CONFIRMING AND MATCHING YOUR INBORN RESOURCES

CHAPTER 7

Confirming Your Discovered Inborn Resources

"Without consultation *and* wise advice, plans are frustrated, but with many counselors they are established and succeed." (Proverbs 15:22 AMP)

It is common for someone to doubt their God-given potential because of the fear of making mistakes. So, how are we going to be sure that the discovery we are making is true or not? Let us consider four tests to confirm whether or not our discovery is true.

Principal's test

Confirmation from those who are leaders or in a position of authority around you is vital. God can use your parents, teachers, and mentors to help guide you and confirm the potential and uniqueness that is inborn in you. Prophet Eli guided the young Samuel to recognise God's voice (1 Samuel 3:1-11). When your vision is blurred, you need these people to guide and enlighten you so you can clearly see a better picture. God may use these leaders to either encourage or discourage you depending on whether this newly discovered potential is from God, or is just your imagination. It may be premature to put the potential into use. These people are placed over you to help you concentrate and cultivate your garden (potential) if God's hand is in it.

Note, an ungodly leader can discourage you from finding and maximizing the use of your inborn resources. King Saul did that to David when he said to him, "You are not able to go against this

Philistine to fight with him, for you are but a youth, and he has been a man of war from his youth" (1 Samuel 17:33).

Do not be discouraged if the people you expect support from do not immediately support you. Remember that a lack of confirmation from those in authority around you is neither a rejection nor a denial. God give them insight not to hurt you, but for your protection.

Patience's test

Your discovery must be able to stand the test of time. If not, then check it, since it may not be an inborn ability. There are times when we want something so bad that we are willing to give up everything else in order to get it. However, when we look back after a week, a month, or a year, we may only faintly remember, or may have completely forgotten, what we were willing to exchange for our whole world. Hence, such an idea is not worth living for if time will erase it in our minds.

Privilege's test

If you have an inborn resource and the timing is right for its use, doors will open for you. If you find yourself forcing doors of opportunity open, then something has yet to be perfected in you. Always remember that God takes care of the doors opening and closing (Isaiah 45:1; Rev. 3:8). God gave Joseph several opportunities to experiment and cultivate his leadership skills in the house of Potiphar (Genesis 39:1-6) and in the prison (Genesis 39:20-23). The door naturally opened through dreams for him at the appointed time and he became the second in command in Egypt (Genesis 41:33-44). God caused a Babylonian king to give scholarship to Daniel and his three friends, so that the gift of wisdom in them could be confirmed and put to use (Daniel 1:1-6,18-21) in fulfilling their life's purpose.

Provision's Test

There is a saying that "Where there is vision, there is provision." Disappointment is not a defeat. It could be part of a purification process. Do not become discouraged by things that appear to be delayed. God may be building a reservoir in you which will be released at a future time. God miraculously used the king of Babylon to finance Nehemiah's ministry, as a confirmation of God's call upon Nehemiah's life (Nehemiah 2:1-8).

Now that we have employed principal, patience, privilege, and provision as tests to confirm our God-given resources, we are now ready to explore principles that will help us maximize the use of any of our discovered resources. However, it is necessary to sit back and think about how the discovered talents can be used to choose possible careers. The importance of matching talents with careers cannot be overemphasized. This is addressed in the next chapter.

CHAPTER 8

Matching Inborn Resources and Careers

The purpose of finding inborn resources is to enable us to match such resources with career opportunities for ourselves and for the social benefit of others. All individuals bring into this world innate talents and uniqueness that may make them better suited for certain careers. Knowing the suitable careers before choosing any educational program, prior to the start of the high school year, would be advantageous. This knowledge would help students choose the appropriate courses that would position them well to live their dreams, or engage in the occupation that suits their talents. Taking this crucial step would prevent many people from wasting time and resources by investing in an educational program that does not position them well for a suitable career.

Note that many people enter into educational programs after graduation, and they begin to find ways to do remedial courses to help them fit into the careers that match their inborn abilities. For instance, I have a friend who is a naturally creative writer. In the twinkling of an eye, she can create a movie in her mind that would last for 2 hours. Unfortunately, she did not understand the importance of matching her talent with a career, and using that connection to prompt the selection of suitable educational courses of study. Instead of pursuing a course in art, she studied electrical engineering. However, her creative writing ability, which she had not been exploring, would not stop being her dream. I have started encouraging her to do some remedial courses in writing.

For easy matching of talents with careers, the information provided in Tables 8.1 to 8.4 are imperative. From the tables, a person can choose any of the careers that match the talents in the corresponding row.

Table 2: Matching careers with talents

Inborn resource	Career path
Administration	Business administrator Project Manager Executive director
Care-giving	Healthcare provider Welfare director, etc
Crafts	Engineering (mechanical, electrical, production, plumbing) Carpentry
Counseling	Counseling Human resources, etc
Creativity	Acting Fashion designing Graphic designing Industrial designing Architecture Animating Advertising, etc
Decorating	Interior designer
Entrepreneur	Business administrator Real estate agent Salesperson
Exhortation	Business administration Public speaking

Table 2: Matching careers with talents

Inborn resource	Career path
Hospitality	Diplomat Public relations office Hotelier Healthcare provider
Leadership	Business administrator Political scientist Advertising executive Managerial position Real estate agent Salesperson Advertising executive Politician
Mentoring	Teacher/Instructor
Music/Singing	Acting Music teaching or directing Singer Song-writing (music composing) Music therapy Art teacher
Organizing (Working with numbers)	Accountant Bank teller Bookkeeper Data entry specialist Insurance Adjuster Logistics Coordinator Payroll clerk

Table 2 (Contd): Matching careers with talents

Organizing (Being organized)	Event planner
	Real estate agent
	Professional organizer
	Merchandiser
	Travel agent
	Project manager
	Tourism officer
	Lawyer
	Editor
	Bookkeeper
	Data entry specialist
	Desk clerk
	Event Planner
	Logistics Coordinator
Public relations	Diplomat
	Public relations office
	Hotelier
Story telling	Author
	Historian
	Multimedia, etc
Teaching	Teaching
	Coaching
	Training
	Pastor/Clergy
Writing	Journalist
	Author, etc

Table 2 (Contd): Matching careers with talents

Solving problems and puzzles	Accountant
	Architect
	Astronaut
	Biologist
	Chemist
	Computer programmer
	Crime scene investigator
	Data security officer
	Medical doctor/Medical sciences
	Engineer
	Financial advisor
	Geneticist
	Meteorologist
	Pharmacist
	Scientist
	Statistician
	Systems analyst
	Veterinarian
	Video game designer
	Web designer

Matching your talents with a career brings relief and less anxiety about your future. The next four chapters deal with how Passion, Optimization, Strategy, and Evaluation are essential to the maximization of your God-given resources.

PART IV

Maximizing Your Discovered Inborn resources:

P-O-S-E

Maximizing Your Discovered Inborn Resources

One day I walked into my Doctoral Professor's office at the University of Idaho. I told him that I would like to defend my project and complete my program at the end of my two and a half years. He was stunned. He looked at me and said "how can you complete a Ph.D. program in less than three years?" I told him that I was finished and reminded him of the enormous amount of work that I had completed. He responded, "But many students who do Chemistry research spend four to five years on it. If you tell people that you completed your Ph.D. program in less than three years, they would think you did a less than substantial job." He later agreed that I could defend my work at the end of the third year.

How did I do it? The work was of a great standard! At least six papers were published in reputable referred journals. Most of my experiments in the laboratory were performed using various instruments. Among them was an instrument that runs for 2 hours per sample. This instrument has an accessory called an auto-sampler which permitted me to set up 12 samples that would last for 24 hours. There were some that only ran for 1 hour. Therefore, I set up many instruments to run simultaneously. It is usually referred to as multitasking. While many students would focus on running their experiment on a single instrument, and move to the other after they had finished with the first, I set up three to four running at the same time. Then I was able to complete a research that would have taken four to five years in less than three years. In short, I maximized my time!

I remembered the words of my Professor then. He used to tell me that I needed to work smart, not only to work hard. A discovered potential doesn't do anyone any good until it is put into use and keeps undergoing continual refining. The more potential (talent) is used, the more it develops, while the less it is used, the more it degenerates. It is by use that such talent will fully function. The discovered potential needs to be maximized. According to a vocabulary dictionary, maximization is the act of rising to the highest possible point. For anyone to increase the functioning of his potential to the greatest possible level of accomplishment, there are action plans that need to be put in place.

With that in mind, we are set to POSE for actions which are:

- **P**assion
- **O**ptimization
- **S**trategy
- **E**valuation

These four actions need to be taken by everyone who wants to fulfill life's purpose through the use of inborn resources. Therefore, the next four chapters address the P-O-S-E principles.

CHAPTER 9
Passion

There are many people who rose from rags to riches, some won a jackpot or lottery, but some became rich because of their PASSION for success. They Pursue Aspiration Sacrificially, Strategically, Industriously, Optimistically, and Nobly. Indeed, everyone must be passionate to utilize his talent. Ezra prepared his heart to know and do the will of God (Ezra 7:10). Remember, you received a gift to benefit others. When this becomes your focus, it gives you a sense of responsibility and helps you to maximize it. To better grasp the meaning and importance of passion, its letters (P-A-S-S-I-O-N) will be used to enhance its understanding.

Pursue: Passion makes us pursue our God-given potential wholeheartedly with all our energy. It makes us not settle for less, but to pursue the best. Passion makes us give up everything to pursue our career and life's purpose. A person with passion will confidently put his or her entire mind to maximizing the use of his or her potential. Our sleeping and waking thoughts would center on pursuing and fulfilling our inborn resources. When you wake up in the morning and you do not feel like doing anything, passion pushes you to take steps to fulfill your dream. It creates the ambition and energy to do what is required in order to excel in the use of your potential.

Aspiration: Maximizing the use of inborn resources makes us turn expectation into aspiration, which is a strong desire to reach a set goal, but aspiration is not enough. Passionate people turn aspiration into action. So a passionate person decides that nothing will serve as a stumbling block on the way up. His or her aspiration is unquenchable. Aspiration makes us stop procrastinating, complaining and living complacently. Instead we look for opportunities to explore and engage in productive activity. There is an old gospel hymn that gives a clear description of the full meaning of aspiration.

> I'm pressing on the upward way,
> New heights I'm gaining every day;
> Still praying as I'm onward bound,
> "Lord, plant my feet on higher ground."
> Refrain
> > Lord, lift me up and let me stand,
> > By faith, on Heaven's table land,
> > A higher plane than I have found;
> > Lord, plant my feet on higher ground.
>
> My heart has no desire to stay
> Where doubts arise and fears dismay;
> Though some may dwell where those abound,
> My prayer, my aim, is higher ground.
>
> I want to live above the world,
> Though Satan's darts at me are hurled;
> For faith has caught the joyful sound,
> The song of saints on higher ground.
>
> I want to scale the utmost height
> And catch a gleam of glory bright;
> But still I'll pray till Heav'n I've found,
> "Lord, plant my feet on higher ground."

Sacrificially: Passion makes us give up whatever keeps us from achieving our goal. It involves sacrificing desires, pleasure, motives, and lusts that draw us away from maximizing our potential. In addition, it helps us to say NO to lesser joys because of the greater glory that awaits us. A person who is driven by passion exhibits self-control and discipline at all times. It makes us discipline our fleshly desires to pursue our goal. It allows no sleep to our eyes, no slumber to our eyelids (Proverbs 6:4). The Psalmist says, "Surely I will not come into the tabernacle of my house, nor go up into my bed; I will not give sleep to mine eyes, *or* slumber to mine eyelids, until I find out a place for the LORD, an habitation for the mighty *God* of Jacob" (Psalm 132:3-5). Being self-controlled is of great value and it is the basis for remaining focused, even in the midst of distractions and pleasure.

Strategically: Passion makes us strictly follow an organized, well-planned course of action with the aim of reaching the envisioned goal. It is all about engaging in critical and strategic thinking about how to maximize a discovered talent or uniqueness. Procrastination is not tolerated because we know that we need to "make hay while the sun shines." We strategically plan to pursue our vision by maximizing the use of our talents and to shine in it by mapping it out step by step. We know that there is a time for everything, a time to give birth to the vision and a time to nurture it to grow. Like a ravenous wolf we will courageously and diligently schedule ourselves to work at the appropriate time. Jesus said, "I must work the works of Him who sent Me while it is day; *the* night is coming when no one can work" (John 9:4 NKJV).

With passion we will plan our life and do all we can to do the right thing at the right time and in the right way. We strategically eliminate every form of hindrance while embracing any step that enhances the fulfillment of our talent.

Industriously: Diligence brings success in life but it is fueled by passion. It is a constant and earnest effort to nurture your talent and to see it to its full development and use. Someone once said that "people who are industrious work energetically, devotedly, and diligently." A lazy person cannot provide for himself. The Bible says, "He becometh poor that dealeth *with* a slack hand: but the hand of the diligent maketh rich" (Proverbs 10:4). "The hand of the diligent shall bear rule: but the slothful shall be under tribute" (Proverbs 12:24).

Nature does not support laziness, but encourages hard work, patience, and perseverance, investing time and energy to see a job through to completion.

An industrious person never retires. Surprisingly, the Jews have no Hebrew word for retirement because God has no plans for any person to retire. This is because productivity is a way of providing for our human needs. So, when an individual retires from work, he or she stops providing for his or her needs and the needs of others. The retired person needs to stay physically and mentally healthy. Needs that could be provided by a retiree are education through mentoring, counseling and consulting. The Apostle Paul admonished the older women (retired) to engage in teaching the younger women how to be managers of their households (Titus 2:3-5). In fact, retirement is an act of refusal to bless humanity with the talents deposited in us. To retire simply means RE-tire - repeating a loss of interest, being bored or tired of something. A person of passion would not be bored or lose interest in maximizing the use of his or her talent.

Remember, retirement is described in this book as a loss of interest. So, it is possible for an individual, whose job involves physical labor like construction engineering, driving a commercial vehicle, and so on to lose interest in the work with old age. However, the truth is that losing interest in such jobs does not mean that the person cannot develop an interest in other jobs. There are many jobs that retired people can engage in to keep themselves busy and active. The Psalmist states that "They will still bear fruit in old age; they will stay fresh and green" (Psalms 92:14 NIV).

Optimistically: When a person discovers his or her God-given resource to fulfill his or her life's purpose, if there is a fire in his or her bones, commonly known as passion, he or she will be enthusiastic about putting it into maximum use. Winston Churchill stated that "an optimist sees the opportunity in every difficulty."

Being optimistic helps you believe that a lily grows best in natural dirt and in slightly acidic soil. Instead of reacting negatively to obstacles that get in the way of developing and maximizing your talent, optimistic people take it positively. They believe that the obstacles are stepping stones to greatness, and help them become resilient. Indeed, they view everything from the angle of possibility.

Optimism makes people of passion sustain their motivation when developing and using their talents. It helps them to see a glorious outcome that others do not see.

Being an optimistic person does not mean that things will always go the way you plan them, but it means that you do not waste your energy if it does not go your way. Optimistic people spend their energy anticipating a positive outcome on whatever they set their minds to do. They don't settle for less. These people always interrupt all forms of internal and external negative trains of thoughts, ideas or suggestions, and quickly realign their thinking and way of life to mirror what they believe. They do not allow any circumstance or failure to hinder them from pursuing their goal. In fact, developing and maximizing their talent becomes a task that must be accomplished.

Nobly: people of passion do not want to lose their integrity. They want to maintain a high moral standard that cannot be ridiculed by any form of scandal as they pursue their aspirations sacrificially, strategically, industriously, and optimistically. They know that a good name is better than gold. They want to reach the top of the ladder of their talent, but they want to get there honorably.

Recall the professional athletes who want to do well in their careers, but compromised their beliefs and values by using performance enhancing drugs. When these athletes were caught, their reputations were destroyed, images tarnished, family embarrassed, and endorsement contracts by big companies were lost because they didn't want to associate with the disgraced athletes.

The place of passion in maximizing our God-given resources is very crucial. It has been explained that passion is the fuel that generates power to pursue goals without giving up or quitting. Passion can be a game changer in the use of resources, and the optimization of resources is of great benefit. This will be considered in the next section.

CHAPTER 10
Optimization

Maximization is enhanced through optimization. Talent optimization deals with the approach taken to minimize or completely remove any redundant practice while maximizing some practices that would enhance the best possible performance. In optimization, you need to ask some heart-probing questions like:

- What are the possibilities that I can attain in my career or talent?
- What are the unmet needs that the use of my career/talent can provide?
- Which areas of my life can I identify to help me break through to success?
- What are the things that I need to do to invest my time and treasure?

Step 1: Find Your TOWS

The approach to take in answering these questions with honesty and sincerity is to consider a car that has a problem which requires the help of a **tow** vehicle to get it to the auto-mechanic shop for repair. So the acronym of TOWS will be used. This is commonly known as SWOT. However, it would be preferable to modify it as TOWS which stands for Threats, Opportunities, Weaknesses, and Strengths. When someone says that he has two kinds of news, bad news and good news, people normally want the bad news first. So it is good to start considering how to optimize what we have by discovering the negatives before the positives.

In talent or career optimization, whatever will prevent you from becoming the best in the use of your talent should be identified. Then the weaknesses that pull you down from climbing the ladder of success in your talent or career must be named. After that, look for the opportunities that currently present themselves to you, or that you envisage will help you grow in your talent or career.

Threats

Threats are the external factors which cloud your mind with all kinds of fear and tell you that you cannot make progress in your pursuit. If you do not discover and deal with them appropriately, they can strangle your strengths and opportunities. Therefore be sincere in naming your fears and any Goliath threatening your David. Some examples of these kinds of threats are an inferiority complex, fear of failure, loneliness, abandonment by people who are close to you, etc.

To identify these threats, do the following exercises:

1. List all the possible barriers that you are currently facing or envisaging that prevent you from taking steps toward achieving your set goal to maximize your talents.

2. List your personal traits that are hurting your career advancement.

3. List the new technologies or techniques that could be helpful in maximizing your talents, without which you could become redundant, but you have not mastered them yet.

4. Identify the people who you think may be threats to you because they are outperforming you.

5. Outline the things that you consider hindrances to achieving your goals

6. List all the professional standards which you think you cannot meet in order to become outstanding in your career/talent.

7. List the challenges of life that could threaten your talent fulfillment.

Opportunities

Opportunities are the situations that make it possible for a person to reach a desirable achievement. They are divine provisions to engage in something better than before. Normally, strengths and weaknesses give birth to opportunities. However, talent or career optimization could dictate the doors of opportunities that might open. For example, if you improve the use of your talent, what opportunities does the future hold for you? In order to identify these opportunities, consider the following exercises:

1. List any skills or techniques (be a new stylist, creativity, innovative ideas, better education, advance technology) which could make you become outstanding in the use of your talent or career.

2. List all the connections (training, trainers) that could help you excel in your talent

3. Research the needs of your world or in the environment around you that may require the use of your talents or careers.

4. Attend conferences and join groups that can help you connect with good mentors, obtain good tips, and open up doors for you to develop your strengths.

Weaknesses

Weaknesses are the negative attitudes which a person has little or no control over. They are defective features that prevent someone from becoming powerful and fruitful. In order for you to discover your weaknesses, a Johari window (Luff and Ingham, 1955) can be employed. All the bad habits you have acquired in life could be discovered within the Johari window. In addition, the lists of the qualifications or training that you need, but don't have, and which are paramount to your success in the use of your talent or career, are your weaknesses.

Strengths

Strengths are the positive attributes which a person has that grant him competitive advantages to succeed in life. They are the inborn powers to resist the internal and external pressures which contend against your forward and upward journey. Strengths, like weaknesses, can also be discovered using a Johari window.

Johari window model

Johari window model is a psychological tool developed in 1955 by Joseph Lutt and Harri Ingham. One of the goals of this model is to become more self aware of one's strengths and weaknesses. Understanding one's weaknesses gives the opportunity to turn them around to strengths. The Johari window has a quadrant which is commonly referred to as the four quarters of the coordinate plane.

The four panes of this window are assumed to contain all the strengths and weaknesses of a person as illustrated in Figure 1. The "arena" pane contains the strengths and weaknesses that are both known to you and to the people around you. The "mask" pane contains the strengths and weaknesses that are only known to you but not to people who are familiar to you.

<table>
<tr><td>Arena
(Open)</td><td>Blind spots</td></tr>
<tr><td>Facade/Mask

(Hidden)</td><td>Unknown</td></tr>
</table>

Johari Window (Luff & Ingham, 1955)

The "blind spots" pane contains the strengths and weaknesses that are known to people around you but are unknown to you. Lastly, the "unknown" pane contains the strengths and weaknesses that are both unknown to you and people around you. These "unknown" potentials can be discovered as you interact and dialogue with people, or face the challenges of life which could bring out these hidden strengths or weaknesses. Remember, the juice of an orange would not come out unless the fruit is pressed.

The strengths and weaknesses of the arena pane could be confirmed by using the mirrors that others are holding through which you view your reflection. For the "blind spots," ask people who are familiar with you and who are from various walks of life to honestly point out your strengths and weaknesses. Don't forget to be sincere when listing your "mask" strengths and weaknesses. Finally, arrange them in the order of frequency. The most frequent are the strengths and weaknesses that you need to tackle.

For the Johari Window, some adjectives are listed from which you can choose to describe yourself. In this book, additional adjectives, phrases or sentences are included to accommodate some weaknesses. They are contained in Tables 3 and 4.

Table 3: Various strengths

Able	Extroverted	Organizational
Accepting	Friendly	Organized
Adaptable	Giving	Patient
Analytical	Happy	Powerful
Believable	Lack of time	Prioritised Kind
Bold	management	Quiet
Brave	Less resources	Reflective
Calm	Love of pleasure	Relaxed
Caring	Helpful	Religious
Cheerful	Idealistic	Respectful
Clever	Independent	Responsive
Communicative	Ingenious	Searching
Complex	Intelligent	Self-assertive
Confident	Interpersonal	Self-conscious
Creative	Introverted	Sensible
Dedicated	Insightful	Spontaneous
Dependable	Knowledgeable	Support system
Determined	Logical	Sympathetic
Disciplined	Loving	Trustworthy
Dignified	Mature	Warm
Empathetic	Modest	Wise
Energetic	Multitasking	Witty
Enthusiastic	Observant	Visionary

Table 4: Various weaknesses

Careless attitude	Negative mindset towards things
Disorganized	Negative work habits
Fear of public speaking	Nervous
Indifferent	Passive
Lazy	Poor at handling stress
Lack of career direction or focus	Poor sleeping habits (waking up late, too much sleep)
Lack confidence in self	Procrastination
Lack of trust in others	Proud
Lack of enough training in the needed aspect of your life	Sentimental
Lack of education	Short temper
Lack of work experience or expertise	Shy
Lack of self-motivation	Silly
	Tense
	Undecided
	Undisciplined

Step 2: Matching, converting and minimizing

After this discovery, you need to use all the information that you have gathered to optimize your performance. There are three important approaches (match, convert and minimize) to turn things around in your favor and for maximum performance.

Matching: Match your strengths to opportunities around you. You have to think and make a decisive effort to match your strengths in the most effective way to your opportunities. Matching your weaknesses to the identified threats gives you some insight into areas where you need to be defensive or offensive, to protect yourself and make decisions on how to overcome the threats.

Conversion: After outlining your weaknesses, you need to convert those weaknesses into strengths, and change the threats into opportunities using all your resources. Remember, nothing is impossible to him who believes. Let your mindset of "not possible" change to "it is possible." Make up your mind to experience a change from weakness to strength. It is possible to turn your weaknesses into strengths. Be courageous and brave, for you are able to do it. Where there is a will, there is always a way. Your decision today will determine your destiny.

It is important that you make up your mind to get an education, or take some training that will help you turn your weaknesses into strengths. If you think you need some career counseling, look for an experienced counselor in the area that needs changing. Within the counseling field there is a solution for every problem.

Be determined. Get ready for a conversion. Someone said, "Proper preparation prevents poor performance." Carry out a survey, then make a plan toward the change and strategically execute the plan. Be determined to give it all it would take for you to turn your identified weaknesses into strengths, and your threats into opportunities.

Proper examination of any of your weaknesses will reveal that each of your weaknesses has an embedded strength. For example, if your weakness is argument, then become an apologist. Instead of being talkative, become a public speaker. Your stubbornness can make you a determined person who will never give up until an assignment is accomplished. In the same way, most threats have some hidden opportunities. Changing your mindset will help you see the opportunities attached to the threats. Winston Churchill, a former British Prime Minister, said, "A pessimist sees the difficulty in every opportunity, but an optimist sees the opportunity in every difficulty."

Minimizing: It is 100% possible to convert your weaknesses into strengths, but if it seems impossible, then minimize the weaknesses by exercising your strengths. Likewise, you can also use your strengths to minimize the threats. Adopt strategies that minimize your weaknesses by taking advantage of the opportunities that present themselves to you, and grow throughout the process. In the same way, you can minimize your weaknesses by upgrading yourself in order to avoid the threats. For example, someone with no college education (weakness) may be threatened with an upcoming appointment termination. However, if the person would upgrade his education by enrolling in part-time school, the threat can be avoided after obtaining a college degree.

The use of TOWS helps us to see the possibility of optimizing our talents and careers. The possibility comes through self-improvement. Learning is a lifelong process which does not stop after college graduation. In fact, there are some who do not even have a college degree, and yet nothing stops them from learning without a classroom. For anyone to optimize his inborn resources with the goal of fulfilling life's purpose, the person needs to keep on learning. Engage in reading books to broaden your knowledge, because the more you read, the more wisdom you gain.

In order to maximize the use of your talent, you do not need to pay for college. You can bring a university of various ideas and intellect into your room. Thank God for the internet and information technology. Acquire and read books that are written on how to improve your specific potential, talents, skills, attitude, integrity, etc. Above all, develop the habit of reading the book of Proverbs in the Bible on a daily basis. Read one chapter per day in addition to your normal Bible reading. It contains only 31 chapters. For any month which contains 30 days, just read an extra chapter on a weekend. Additionally, for February which contains 28 days, just read an extra chapter on three weekends. The book of Proverbs contains a lot of wisdom for living and for optimizing the use of inborn resources to fulfill life's purpose. It will make you wise.

Another aspect of education is to learn from good mentors. He who walks with the wise will become wise (Proverbs 13:20). Get a good mentor or friend who will always be there to encourage you and also provide feedback and feedforward (Proverbs 27:17; Ecclesiastes 4:9-12). Feedback focuses on rating and judging a person's past performance while feedforward focuses on future development and encourages people to see opportunities for growth. If you do not have the opportunity to meet a desired person to mentor you, the easiest and quickest approach is to get almost all the books and tapes that such a person authored. Then read or listen to them until you understand every single point in them.

You are also to learn from your past experiences, bad or good. See them as opportunities to learn and grow in order to optimize your potential.

Additionally, self-improvement involves letting go and downsizing. In industry, the purpose of optimization is to reduce the cost of production while increasing the profit. Likewise, the principle of downsizing must not be removed from our lives. It is another way to optimize our capacity. God told Gideon to downsize his army from 30,000 to 300. Anything that would bring discouragement and encourage laziness is to be removed, while anything that would encourage a winning mindset is to be retained.

Talent, treasure, and time wastage can be prevented when there is an effective optimization of all the available resources to maximize your God-given potential. This makes every effort more efficient. Any practice and way of life that does not efficiently contribute to growing your talents and gifts should be eliminated or it may render the talents or gifts sterile, and prevent the positive contribution of your talents.

In addition, another aspect of self-improvement deals with time management. Train yourself to become a good timekeeper. Effective time management makes a person more productive, less stressed, and helps him or her accomplish more on his or her agenda each day. In order to be an effective time manager, you must know how to set your priorities straight. Focus on the most important activities on your to-do-list. Spending more time on activities that may be urgent is crucial to productivity.

Once the to-do list is in place, cultivate the habit of saying NO to any pop-up activities that do not fit into the already set priorities. Effective time management entails scheduling your time appropriately. Avoiding any form of distraction helps to effectively manage time. In this present generation, distractions are everywhere. Social media (like Facebook, Twitter, WhatsApp, etc.), movies, and cell phone (texting and talking) could distract us from focusing on what matters. The best practical step to avoid their distractions is to put your cell phone on silent mode and disable your social media when you are set to work. You too must make up your mind not to be distracted.

Effective time management helps with the avoidance of multitasking. There is a slogan which says, "Jack of all trades and master of none." Learn to take one step at a time for easy coordination. Taking two steps at a time may make you lose your balance.

As we conclude on how to optimize the use of our inborn resources, the following question and answer on Per Person Productivity summarises all that we have considered so far on optimization.

Don Clifton, the founder of StrengthsFinder, was once asked about how to turn talent into outcomes as cited Ruhlman (2014) explained. He made it clear that if only identifying strengths and talents could unlock human potential, it would be great. He then answered the question by encouraging people to consider the opportunity to leverage talent as represented in the following equation:

$$PPP = T(R + E + F)$$

Where PPP = Per Person Productivity

    T = Talent

    R = Relationship

    E = Expectation

    F = Feedback/Rewards/Recognition

The talent is the multiplier. The three key components that are in the parenthesis are very important to transforming talent into wonderful outcomes. If you have a great talent but the summation of the other three components is low, your per person productivity will be low. For example, putting the four factors on a scale of 10:

Example 1: when talent is 10, relation is 10, expectation (goal is clear) is 10 and reward (feedback is prompt) is 10, per person productivity will be 300.

Example 2: when talent is 10, relation is 1, expectation is 1 and reward is 1, per person productivity will be 30.

Example 3: when talent is 1, relation is 10, expectation (goal is clear) is 10 and reward is 10 (feedback is prompt), per person productivity will be 30.

The three components inside the parentheses could be likened to the culture that allows the talent to germinate, grow, and flower. The reason for discovering talent is to position it according to what it can do, not what it cannot do and then to continually think about how we can leverage that talent to excel in life and fulfill our life's purpose.

Several points were addressed with the goal of optimizing all the available resources to maximize the use of talents. The ways to match strengths to opportunities, convert weaknesses into strengths, and threats into opportunities were explained. In addition, how to minimize weaknesses by exercising strengths, and how to minimize threats by using strengths were described. Efficient optimization will be effective when a sound strategic plan is in place, which is the point considered in the next chapter.

CHAPTER 11
Strategy

Strategic planning for the maximization of any discovered talent requires setting goals before the talented can excel. Clear goals and plans to achieve the goals for each day must be set before the start of the day's activities. In the process of setting up the plan, ask yourself, "how will I achieve my goals?" "How can I use my inborn resources to fulfill my life's purpose?" "How will I go from good to great, better to best, expansion to explosion?" Answering these questions will help you come up with a detailed plan of how you can improve on your strengths and overcome your weaknesses, as well as turning your threats into opportunities in order to maximize the use of your talent. Do not rush out to face each day's work without drafting a plan on what to do and how to do it. Rushing out without a plan will only lead to failure or disappointment. Being diligent is great, but it is only rewarding, productive, and brings abundance if a well-structured plan is put in place before exerting too much energy. Do not struggle through life. Instead soar through life, which can only happen when you have a workable plan. A hardworking person who fails to slow down in order to take his or her time is actually planning to fail. So do not act in impatience and haste when a well-structured plan is not in place. It only leads to poverty. If your great ideas are devoid of action, your plans will turn to delusion. So draw up a workable strategic plan.

Steps to Effective Strategic Planning

Determine your target: A result-oriented strategy involves setting up proper goals. Ask yourself, what are my targets? What is the big picture that I envision? What goal do I want to reach? What are my long term and short term goals?

Define S-M-A-R-T Goals: It is important to write down on paper what you want to accomplish. It will serve as a quick and daily reminder of what ought to be completed next. The question is, how do we set goals that make sense? Let us consider five steps to setting winning goals by using an acronym for S.M.A.R.T.

Step #1: Specific

For any person to use and maximize their inborn resources, their talent, or uniqueness, the first thing is to set specific goals. Be specific in what you want to achieve. The more simple, concise and specific you are in describing what you want, the greater the possibility will be of achieving your goal. Jesus asked the blind Bartimaeus for his specific goal, not just a general goal of "have mercy on me." That is too broad and generic. Bartimaeus replied to Jesus that "I want to see again" (Mark 10:46-52). That is specific and straightforward.

Therefore, provide enough detail so that there is no uncertainty as to what you should be doing with the set goals. For example, if you discover that you have a musical talent, you need to set a general goal of allocating 5 or 10 hours per week and register for a music class where you can learn music. Just allocating 10 hours per week is not specific enough. You have to break it down to one hour and 25 minutes per day, for example. It is necessary to put an exact figure on it.

Step #2: Meaningful and Measurable

You have to set goals that are meaningful and measurable. If your goal is not meaningful, you have nothing to pursue, and no task to carry out. The Apostle Paul asked the Corinthian believers, "For if the trumpet makes an uncertain sound, who will prepare for battle?" (1 Corinthians 14:8 NKJV). In the same manner, if your goal makes an uncertain sound, you will not know what to pursue and so you will not be able to achieve it. There must be a concrete standard to which you can compare it. For example, taking the case of musical talent, decide that by one year from now, you will want to be able to read notes and sing classical music.

Step #3: Attainable and Achievable

Is the goal achievable or attainable? This is not about using the common proverbial statement of "where there is a will, there is always a way." Many people set vague goals that cannot be achieved in the allotted time. When setting a goal, ask yourself if you can achieve this goal at the set time? Setting a 10 year goal is great, but you have to break it down into shorter segments. It is absurd to set a goal of becoming a professional musician within 6 months. You will just stress yourself out and break down. Let your short-term goal be something within your reach, but it should not be so simple that it does not require effort and sweat.

Step #4: Realistic and Relevant

Set goals that are realistic and relevant in order to maximize your inborn resources. Setting a goal with the aim of maximizing your discovered God-given resource should not be burdensome, but should be in line and in harmony with what you want to be doing. Remember, God gives you the talent to be a witness for Him. So when you discover that you have musical talent, your goal should not be to compete with ungodly musicians. Your goal should be to glorify God.

Step #5: Time-oriented

Your goals should be time-oriented. Tie every goal to a specific time period for its accomplishment. This will help you to measure each goal at a specific time.

After setting SMART goals, each of the goals must be given the required resources of time, money, sacrifice, etc. When there is no provision for resources, it becomes difficult for a vision to be accomplished. Once action plans have been drafted, break them down into short-term, medium-term and long-term goals. Then, begin with the short-term goals and work progressively towards the long-term ones. You have to take action and not think too hard about the HOW. Remember, the hand of the diligent shall be made fat (Proverbs 13:4).

Draft prioritized needs: Many people who want to maximize their potential fail to list their goals in order of importance and priority. The most important things have to be done first, which is not necessarily the easiest or even the most urgent.

Devise a plan: Alan Lakein states that "planning is bringing the future into the present so that you can do something about it now." Don't make the mistake of not having a plan to maximize your talent. Creating quantity and quality time to engage in effective planning is not a waste of time. There is no way you can maximize your potential when you fail to have a plan in place. No one plans to fail, but many fail to plan. Proper preparation prevents poor performance, while poor preparation precedes poor performance. So have a good plan in place.

The procedures to employ in embarking on strategic planning, goal setting and plans to carry out the goals, have been addressed. In order to fine-tune the plan to accomplish the goal, evaluation is important. This is dealt with in the next chapter.

Chapter 12

Evaluation

Most of the Science and Mathematics textbooks have some exercises at the end of every topic or chapter. This is to give students an opportunity to evaluate themselves after studying each topic. In fact, the practice of evaluation dates back to the book of Genesis 1. At the end of each creation day, God consistently evaluated His work. So we must evaluate every step we take in following the activities we planned towards the achievement of each set of goals. The main reasons for conducting an evaluation is to obtain results, to gain insight about what is going on, and then make a decision based on the data collected for improvement and future activities.

Evaluation should be an ongoing process that assesses the strengths, weaknesses, and performance of a set goal, and then drafts ways to improve it based on the outcome. In order to maximize the use of your God-given resource, evaluation is very important. According to MEERA, "evaluation is a periodic and continuous process of collecting and analyzing information about a program's activities, characteristics, and outcomes." This is done with the aim of using the resulting information to determine whether you are effectively carrying out the already planned activities, and to what extent the objectives have been accomplished.

The progress of every set goal must be evaluated. For anyone to maximize the fulfillment of a career or talent he must engage in the strategy of evaluating his work. How far have I gone? Why does the result look that way? Have I made any progress at all?

What challenges have I encountered and how have I overcome them?

After a thorough evaluation has been done, you have to embrace whatever change the evaluation outcome suggests. Life is not static. To maximize the use of your inborn resources and fulfill life's purpose, you must embrace change and be ready to change any unprofitable tactic. When you start working on a goal using a specific approach, and you are not making headway, repeating the approach will only continue to end in failure. You need to make an adjustment to the approach. Your method may be faulty and need change. Keep on modifying your goals if necessary. Instead of focusing on the big picture, consider how each daily goal will contribute to the development of your inborn resources. There are two broad categories of evaluations, namely formative and summative.

Evaluations conducted during the development of a program with the aim of understanding the next step of action is called formative assessment. Formative evaluations help you identify your strengths and weaknesses, and concentrate more on the areas that need improvement. MEERA suggested that "summative evaluations should be completed once your programs are well established, and will tell you to what extent the program has achieved its goals."

Tasks are assessed at the end of a working cycle, and findings are usually used to make decision on the possibility of adopting, continuing, discontinuing, or modifying a program for improvement. Evaluation is very essential to maximize potential as it helps to:

- ensure that goals are met
- identify successes and failures

- identify problems and weakness so they can be addressed
- provide information to promote advancement
- identify needs for further training and development

Evaluation is crucial in monitoring progress and helpful with knowing what to remove, retain, and refine while working toward accomplishing a set goal. So far, the inborn resources have been discovered using Potential, Uniqueness, and Reflection. In addition, the approaches to maximize the discovered resources using Passion, Optimization, Strategy, and Evaluation were explained. Matching talents with careers is helpful in determining which academic training a person should pursue. We need to know how to go forward using our resources to fulfill life's purpose. This will be considered next.

PART V

GOING FORWARD

CHAPTER 13

What Next?

There are many unique talents that were never discovered or used before the talented departed this world. Also, there are many unique talents that were discovered but never fully maximized. The desire to discover, develop, and make good use of your inborn resources is powerful. Indeed, "where there is no vision, the people perish" (Proverbs 29:18). As good as a vision is, when it does not get off the ground and soar into the sky, it benefits no one. Why build an airplane that cannot fly? It is very important to discover your unique talents, but it is more important to make full use of such unique talents and fully optimize them.

Now that you have followed the practical steps to discover, develop, and maximize your talents and uniqueness, there are some secrets that will help you propel your flight to the expected destination.

Self Identification: Bear in mind that you are created to be creative, born to bloom and shine. Know for sure that you are born with at least one talent and unique quality.

Single Principle
   a. Be a man or woman of a single eye. Remain focused and don't allow any form of distraction.
   b. Be a man or woman of a single goal. There are many things to pursue in life but not all are profitable or will help you use your talents and uniqueness.

c. Be ready to give all it will take to reach your goal without allowing any form of distraction.

Strong Determination

Strong determination involves:

a. Be ready to pay the price of following your dream of using and maximizing your talent and uniqueness until you become an expert at it and a benefit to your generation.

b. Refuse to be distracted from achieving your goal.

c. Reject every form of pleasure in the present while fully keeping your body under control.

d. Deprive yourself of some things that may not necessarily be bad but will not contribute to the achievement of your goal.

e. Renounce every dream killer.

Dear reader, I hope you have had a good and pleasant journey up to this point. Arrival at the final airport of a flight is not the end; you need to enter the city of your destination and enjoy all its blessings. Please don't settle for less, and refuse to be stagnant. There is no limit to what you can do with your talents and uniqueness. Remember, you are born to bloom. I hope that you have allowed this book to help you discover your talents and uniqueness so that you can be useful to yourself and to your world.

At this point, I would like to inform you that all human beings are entitled to enjoy the resources that the Creator has deposited in them without any exemption. Read these quotes: "This is what God does. He gives his best - the sun to warm and the rain to nourish - to everyone, regardless: the good and bad, the nice and nasty" [people] (Matthew 5:45 MSG).

God spoke: "Let us make human beings in our image, make them

reflecting our nature

So they can be responsible for the fish in the sea,

the birds in the air, the cattle,

And, yes, Earth itself,

and every animal that moves on the face of Earth."

God created human beings;

he created them godlike,

Reflecting God's nature.

He created them male and female.

God blessed them:

"Prosper! Reproduce! Fill Earth! Take charge!

Be responsible for fish in the sea and birds in the air,

for every living thing that moves on the face of Earth." (Genesis 1:26-28 MSG)

Everything that God created in this world and in us is to help us accomplish great success in life. Indeed, there are different levels of accomplishment in life. There are people who operate at the minimum, medium, or maximum level. The people who operate at the minimum level are those who only have a smell of the sweetness of their greatness. However, operating at the medium level allows a person to enjoy the blessings of their talents and uniqueness to a limited extent. The fullness of blessings comes when a person operates at the maximum level.

I read an article about the survival of animals and plants based on the creation account in the book of Genesis. In this account, the land was commanded to produce vegetation. Therefore, "the land produced vegetation: plants bearing seed according to their kinds and trees bearing fruit with seed in it according to their kinds"

(Genesis 1:20-21 NIV). In addition, "the waters teem with fish and other life. So God created great sea animals and every sort of fish" (Genesis 1:20-21 TLB). Thereafter, "God said, Let us make a man, someone like ourselves, to be the master of all life upon the earth and in the skies and in the seas." "The time came when the Lord God formed a man's body from the dust of the ground and breathed into it the breath of life. And man became a living person" (Genesis 1:26; 2:7 TLB). The creation of these three living things is unique. Plants can only survive for a short time without soil because they were brought forth by the soil. Fish can only survive for a short time without water because they were made to display their swimming and survival capability in water. Likewise, human beings can only operate in the use of their God-given resources at minimal or medium levels without the giver of those inborn resources.

Remember, the ultimate goal of your existence on earth is to endorse God by glorifying Him and equipping others to benefit mankind. Operation at the maximum level in the use of your talents and uniqueness becomes achievable when you are connected to your Creator who breathes the breath of life inside of you. God who designed and created you with about 86 billion cells in your brain does not want you to detach from him. He loves you and me so much that He wants us to remain connected to Him so that we can operate our talents at the maximum level to fulfill our life's purpose. No wonder He sent Jesus Christ to serve as a bridge between Him and human beings. Read this quote from John 15:1-5 (NKJV):

"I am the true vine, and My Father is the vinedresser.

Every branch in Me that does not bear fruit He takes

away; and every branch that bears fruit He prunes, that it may bear more fruit. You are already clean because of the word which I have spoken to you. Abide in Me, and I in you. As the branch cannot bear fruit of itself, unless it abides in the vine, neither can you, unless you abide in Me. I am the vine, you are the branches. He who abides in Me, and I in him, bears much fruit; for without Me you can do nothing."

When you reconnect and remain connected with God through Jesus Christ, the use of your talents and uniqueness will produce fruits and lasting fruit (John 15:5,8,16). It is quite simple to take the step. The first thing to do is to believe that Christ came to die for our sin. The next step is to acknowledge that without God, we will not be able to operate at the maximum level. The final step is to surrender to Him and make Him the Captain of our life. Ask God to forgive your sins and give you the grace to follow His instructions on daily basis. Don't forget, your ROAD TO SUCCESS IS UNDER CONSTRUCTION. You can begin a new life with God today.

Glossary

Adage: a proverb or short statement that expresses a general truth.

Career: an occupation, vocation, profession, job, employment that a person undertakes for a long period which also serves as a source of income.

Endorsing God: people's talents and uniqueness are public proof of God's incomprehensible creative design of human beings. Everyone is formed to showcase (witness to) the greatness and glory of God.

Equipping others: every individual's responsibility is to help others discover and put to use their own natural ability.

Feedback: suggestions given which focus on rating and judging a person's past performance of a task

Feedforward: suggestions given which focus on future development and encourage people to see opportunities for growth.

Inborn resources: refer to talents and uniqueness that are part of the makeup of a person.

Life's purpose: the primary reason for human existence in the world. It is the principal motivating aim of the Creator of life for all human beings.

Need-driven activities: activities that improve the lives of other people and testify to the great work of God's creation.

Passion: something that a person enjoys doing, that makes the person lose track of time and that the person is excited to talk about.

Potential: the natural ability commonly referred to as talent that lies within a person, which is developed through use to benefit humanity.

Puff-puff: African doughnut bites.

Purpose: an expansion of the word purpose in this book is written as **P**otential, **U**niqueness, **R**eflection, **P**assion, **O**ptimization, **S**trategy, **E**valuation.

Reflection: recalling the past to determine a pattern for future reference.

Talent optimization: approach taken to minimize or completely remove any redundant practice while maximizing some practices that would enhance the best possible performance

Talents: natural ability that makes a person good at doing something.

Uniqueness: natural ability that is the only one of its kind. This differs from talent. Many people can have the same talent, but the uniqueness displayed in talent is a fingerprint of its possessor.

Venn diagram: a concept mapping approach to find a possible logical common ground among talents, passion, and human needs.

REFERENCES

Cherbuin, N., and Brinkman, C. (2006). Hemispheric interactions are different in left-handed individuals. *Neuropsychology, 20,* 700-707. doi: 10.1037/0894-4105.20.6.700

Dewey, J. (2019). *Democracy and Education an Introduction to the Philosophy of Education.* New York: Macmillan.

Doran, G. T. (1981). There's a S.M.A.R.T. way to write management's goals and objectives. *Management Review (AMA FORUM)* 70, 11:35–36.

Jens (2017). Purpose Venn Diagram. Retrieved from http://www.humanbusiness.eu/ purpose-venn-diagram/

Lakein, A. (1973). *How to Get Control of Your Time and Your Life.* New York City.

Paringit, D. (2016). Turn your weaknesses into strengths. *Skills Development.* Retrieved from https://careerbuzz.prosky.co/articles/6-steps-to-turning-your-weakness-into-your-greatest-strengths

Plato. 1955. *Republic.* (Jowett B., Trans.). *The Project Gutenberg EBook of The Republic by Plato. Release Date: August 27, 2008 [EBook #1497]. Last Updated: June 22, 2016. Retrieved from https://www.gutenberg.org/files/1497/1497-h/1497-h.htm#link2H_INTR*

Rees, E. (2008). S.H.A.P.E.: Finding and fulfilling your unique purpose for life. ISBN-13: 978-0310292487. Zondervan, Michigan, United States.

Ruhlman, J. (2014). Varsity management: A formula for maximizing potential. *Cliftonstrengths* August 6, 2014.

https://www.gallup.com/cliftonstrengths/en/251324/varsity-management-formula-maximizing-potential.aspx

Zint, M. (n.d.). Evaluation: What is it and why do it? A publication of My Environmental Education Evaluation Resource Assistant Retrieved on December 11, 2019 from http://meera.snre.umich.edu/evaluation-what-it-and-why-do-it#good

Books written by Dr. James Fabiyi

1. Hold the Fort — Overcoming Temptations
2. Understanding Your Identity in Christ